TOM WELLS

Tom is a playwright. He lives in Hull and is an Associate Artist of Middle Child.

Plays include *Me, As A Penguin* (West Yorkshire Playhouse/ Arcola); *The Kitchen Sink* (Bush); *Jumpers for Goalposts* (Paines Plough/Watford Palace/Hull Truck); *Cosmic* (Root Theatre/Ros Terry); *Folk* (Birmingham Rep/Watford Palace/ Hull Truck); *Broken Biscuits* (Paines Plough/Live Theatre) and *Stuff* (National Theatre Connections).

Other work includes *Jonesy* and *Great North Run* (BBC Radio 4); *Drip* with music by Matthew Robins (Script Club/Boundless); *Ben & Lump* (Touchpaper/Channel 4) and pantos for the Lyric Hammersmith and Middle Child, Hull.

Tom Wells

BIG BIG SKY

NICK HERN BOOKS
London
www.nickhernbooks.co.uk

A Nick Hern Book

Big Big Sky first published in Great Britain in 2021 as a paperback original by Nick Hern Books Limited, The Glasshouse, 49a Goldhawk Road, London W12 8QP

Big Big Sky copyright © 2021 Tom Wells

Tom Wells has asserted his moral right to be identified as the author of this work

Cover image: © iStock.com/redtea

Designed and typeset by Nick Hern Books, London
Printed in the UK by Mimeo Ltd, Huntingdon, Cambridgeshire PE29 6XX

A CIP catalogue record for this book is available from the British Library

ISBN 978 1 83904 018 4

Woodland
CARBON
www.woodlandcarbon.co.uk
NICK HERN BOOKS
Printed on Carbon Captured paper

Big Big Sky was first performed at Hampstead Theatre Downstairs, London, on 30 July 2021. The cast was as follows:

ANGIE	Jennifer Daley
LAUREN	Jessica Jolleys
ED	Sam Newton
DENNIS	Matt Sutton

Director	Tessa Walker
Designer	Bob Bailey
Design Associate	Roisin Martindale
Lighting Designer	Jai Morjaria
Sound Designer	Laura Howard

For Jean Spencer and Matthew Wells,
with love

Characters

ANGIE, *forties*
DENNIS, *forties*
LAUREN, *nineteen*
ED, *twenty-one*

Setting

Angie's café in Kilnsea, on the corner of Kilnsea beach and the road to Spurn.

Clean and warm with sturdy wooden benches and tables, a glass cabinet on the counter full of cakes and scones and sandwiches, cans of pop, Mars bars at the side, soup and pasties and beans keeping warm at the back.

A board on the wall is covered in notices. They're quite old.

Some wooden gulls hang from the ceiling.

This text went to press before the end of rehearsals and so may differ slightly from the play as performed.

Autumn

1.

Saturday. Dusk.

LAUREN *drags the sign in from outside, a big sandwich board saying 'Café Open', and shuts the door. She leans the sign against the wall.*

ANGIE *comes out of the kitchen.*

ANGIE. Are we done?

LAUREN. Fingers crossed.

> LAUREN *looks through the window.*
>
> Quite a big family in the car park – people carrier, two dogs – thought if we look closed when they get here, might let us off the hook a bit.

ANGIE. Did they look hungry?

LAUREN. Hard to tell, isn't it, under all the fleeces. Need something we can just pass them Mars bars through the door.

ANGIE. Plan.

LAUREN. Reckon they got the hint anyway.

ANGIE. Did you glare?

LAUREN. Not much. A bit. It's sort of just my face. Best crack on.

ANGIE. Have a rest for a minute.

LAUREN. It's fine.

ANGIE. Hardly stopped since we opened.

LAUREN. Neither have you.

ANGIE. There's oat slice left. If you fancied a bit of oat slice.

LAUREN. I'm honestly fine, Angie.

ANGIE. Got a long night still to –

LAUREN. Exactly. And to be honest, I'm shitting myself a bit, so I feel like the best thing to do is just get all cleared up here, grab my stuff, maybe we can set off a bit early if that's okay? So I can run through a couple of the songs once we get to the actual, once we're there.

ANGIE. We'll get cleared up, get Neil picked up, get there soon as. Apparently he's wearing a cowboy hat.

LAUREN. Course he is.

ANGIE *spots something out the window.*

ANGIE. And here's your dad.

LAUREN. Oh for –

DENNIS *enters.*

DENNIS. Evening.

LAUREN. Every time.

ANGIE. Hello, Dennis.

LAUREN. Every. Flipping –

DENNIS. What you on about: 'every time'?

LAUREN. Every time we shut up, Dad.

DENNIS. Don't be daft.

LAUREN. It's been literally two minutes since I dragged that bloody sign in, you're here to hoover up the leftovers, for free.

DENNIS. Not true, but.

LAUREN. Right.

DENNIS. I'm actually here for two very particular reasons, neither of which involves hoovering up the leftovers.

ANGIE. You sure, Dennis? There's still a pasty left, beans, if you fancy?

DENNIS. Well.

DENNIS *thinks*.

If there's beans.

LAUREN *and* ANGIE *share a look*.

But just to be clear: that's not why I'm here.

ANGIE. Here you are then.

ANGIE *passes* DENNIS *a pasty and beans*.

DENNIS. Cheers, Angie. Lovely.

He digs in.

You can take that face off you and all.

LAUREN. Can I?

DENNIS. Lot on my plate today.

LAUREN. Lot of beans.

They smile.

I'm sorry, Dad, but, bit of a rush, I'll have to clear up round you.

LAUREN *gets on*.

DENNIS. What are you in a rush for?

LAUREN. Nowt. Life.

DENNIS. Well like I say, I've just got a couple of things to –

LAUREN. Dad, you've got your pasty, don't have to pretend –

DENNIS. I do have a couple of things.

LAUREN. Like what?

DENNIS. Well, one: said I'd give you this, in case you can put it up somewhere.

DENNIS *takes a poster out of his bag*.

It's a poster. It's for, um –

LAUREN *is still wiping tables*.

LAUREN. Yep, course, just pop it on the board. It's magnetic but there's magnets.

DENNIS. And two: meant to be meeting this lad. Ed. Said he'd be here at five so he's a bit late actually but.

LAUREN. Who's Ed?

DENNIS. This lad I'm meeting.

LAUREN. Yeah but how come?

DENNIS. Oh. I've rented out your room.

LAUREN *stops wiping tables*.

LAUREN. Um. What?

DENNIS. Your old room.

Well you don't need it any more, do you?

LAUREN. No but –

DENNIS. Exactly. And, bit of extra cash, always handy, isn't it?

LAUREN. I haven't finished emptying it though. All my stuff. Only moved out on Thursday.

DENNIS. Mentioned it down the pub, started telling me about this website: Airbnb. So I put it on, uploaded it to the website, your room – I mean, the room – thinking maybe someone'll want it in the summer, plenty of time to get it sort of up to scratch, clear it out, maybe a lick of paint what have you.

LAUREN. What have you done with my stuff?

DENNIS. Your stuff's fine, love. It's in bin bags in the shed.

LAUREN. Dad.

DENNIS. Next thing I know this lad –

LAUREN. Ed.

DENNIS. He's rented it out for the weekend. Just like that. I've had to sort it out, sharpish. That's today.

LAUREN. No I mean –

DENNIS. More Febreze involved than I expected but.

LAUREN. Dad. Ed.

LAUREN *nods at the door*.

DENNIS. Oh.

ED is opening it slowly.

ED. Um, hiya, sorry to, to barge in I just, I know it says closed but, you're all shut up but, looking for, um...

He looks at a scrap of paper.

Dennis?

Said to meet him here. So I am doing. Hopefully.

DENNIS. That's me.

ED. Oh brilliant. Ed.

He smiles, shakes DENNIS's hand.

DENNIS. Just finishing up here, then I'll...

ED. Course, course, no rush.

DENNIS doesn't rush.

ED looks to ANGIE and LAUREN.

Smiles.

Ed.

ANGIE. I'm Angie. This is Lauren.

LAUREN. Hey.

A moment.

ANGIE. D'you fancy a hot drink, Ed? Cup of tea?

ED. Oh um. Have you got, peppermint tea? That's just, that's mostly what I drink really.

ANGIE. Oh I don't know, er...

ANGIE checks.

We've run out, love.

ED. Not to worry then.

ED looks at DENNIS.

DENNIS is still eating.

ANGIE. You can still come in for a bit, honestly.

ED. I'm all muddy, is the thing. My boots and that.

ANGIE. Don't worry.

ED. I'll leave marks.

ANGIE. Everyone leaves marks.

ED. And you're all shut up, so...

ED smiles.

LAUREN. Dad.

DENNIS. What's up now?

LAUREN. Think Ed could do to get to his room.

ED. Only if it's not too much, I mean, there's no, no rush.

DENNIS. Just finish this.

He tucks in again.

ED. Course. Course.

DENNIS. And then actually I was off to give you all the info about this.

DENNIS *indicates the poster.*

In case people ask.

LAUREN *sighs.*

What?

LAUREN. We already know about it. Honestly, Dad, we've had Kim and Phil showing us their close-ups of Arctic warblers all afternoon.

DENNIS. There's Arctic warblers about?

ANGIE. Just this morning. Pair. Lovely.

DENNIS. You've seen them?

ANGIE *smiles.*

ED. Oh weren't they just...?

ED *looks delighted.*

DENNIS. *You've* seen them?

LAUREN. I'm sure Kim and Phil will be at the pub, delighted to show you their Arctic warblers, Dad. Photos of. To celebrate your sudden and, can I just say, quite unexpected birdwatching obsession.

DENNIS. Alright.

LAUREN. Even though you've lived here forty-five years, never shown the slightest bit of interest.

DENNIS. Alright.

LAUREN. I move out, you put my room on Airbnb, suddenly you're a birdwatcher. It is a bit weird, Dad.

DENNIS. My new leaf, isn't it?

LAUREN. Can I just check: are you having a nervous breakdown?

DENNIS. Lauren.

LAUREN. Are you though?

DENNIS. Just trying some new stuff.

LAUREN. Seems like the sort of thing you'd do if you were having a nervous breakdown.

DENNIS. I'm not having a nervous breakdown.

LAUREN. Not not having one though, I reckon. Well. Not a breakdown but. Bit lonely or something. Quite lonely. Very, very lonely.

DENNIS. Lauren.

LAUREN. Like it's quite a big thing for me to move out. It is though. When you're not used to being on your own. With your thoughts and that. Like there was three of us and then… Then there was two of us for a bit. And now… Just you.

DENNIS *is a bit hurt.*

DENNIS. You finished?

LAUREN *isn't finished.*

LAUREN. Quite a big thing to clear all my stuff into the shed, Dad. Just saying. Join Airbnb.

Speaking of which: Ed.

And me and Angie are in a bit of a rush to get cleared up, get on our way so...

DENNIS. I'm finishing. My beans.

DENNIS *goes back to his beans.*

LAUREN *gives her dad a look, goes back to cleaning.*

ED *doesn't know what to do. He looks around.*

ED. Lovely in here.

ANGIE. Cheers, love.

ED. Wouldn't've worried about packing my sandwiches if I'd known.

ANGIE *smiles, carries on clearing food away.*

Bit risky though, isn't it?

Just sort of turning up to an isolated peninsula in the North Sea without any sandwiches.

Especially now, cos of... Like I am a bit limited really, now, cos of...

ANGIE *doesn't understand.*

ANGIE. Cos of...?

ED. Oh, I just, um... It's sort of... Not to worry.

ED *shakes his head, changes the subject.*

First time here.

Kilnsea, I mean. Spurn.

ANGIE. Know for next time.

ED. Definitely. Definitely.

ANGIE *pops some oat slice in a paper bag.*

ANGIE. Maybe pop this in your bag, for later.

ED. Oh, Angie, thank you, that's so kind but I actually –

ANGIE. Once the sign's in, it's a free-for-all. Saves me taking it home.

ED. Crikey. Wow. Thank you. But, thing is, I'm actually, I'm vegan so. So unless it's vegan I won't be able to. I can't um.

But, thank you.

ANGIE. Love, you should've said.

ED. Trying not to be that person who's like 'I'm a vegan' all the time. Trying not to be him. But, like, I am a vegan, so. All the time, so. So that makes it harder, really.

ANGIE. I've got vegan brownies if they might...?

ED. Oh. Yeah. That'd be, they sound lovely.

ANGIE puts a couple in a bag.

ANGIE. They're a bit wonky but aren't we all?

ED beams.

ED (*quietly*). Thank you.

A moment.

LAUREN. Dad?

DENNIS is still eating.

DENNIS. Nearly done.

LAUREN glares. DENNIS glares back.

ANGIE smiles at ED.

ANGIE. What's brought you here then?

ED. Oh, er. Research mission. Yeah. Or, that's made it sound a bit exciting, and it isn't exciting really, like at all. Well, exciting for me but... I mean, new socks are exciting for me, so...

Applied for, for a job here. Tern Warden.

ANGIE. Oh right.

ED. Yeah.

Like my dream job actually so...

You get to look after the little terns – it's a breed of tern, not just... I mean all terns are quite little but. But you probably know that already, living here and that. Sorry. Don't know why I'm... Anyway. You get to look after them from when they're first building their nests, on the sand, on the dunes to when they're flying off sort of, the babies and that, first time migrating. And if you get it right they'll come back the next year, build their nests again, even more of them. So: proper conservation, isn't it? Hands-on. Outdoors. Fresh air. And you're part of, like, the little terns have been nesting here, coming back every year, for like: decades so... Flipping ages so... Cos they know it's, like they know they'll be safe here, looked after, cared for. So you get to be a little bit of that, a little link in the chain I suppose, which feels... Well. Nice to be part of something bigger than just you, isn't it? I think anyway, so.

Interview's Monday. Monday morning.

But I thought if I had a good explore first, get the lie of the land a bit, I could have some stuff to say and that, for in the interview. Like: local knowledge.

ANGIE. Good plan.

ED. Maybe think of a few ideas too, I thought. Stuff I could bring to the job.

LAUREN. Like what?

ED. Oh. I dunno. Spose: I'm quite good at fencing? As in, like, putting up, mending fences. Not like swordfighting fencing. Don't know how good I am at that. Not very, I expect. But, um...

I've forgotten...

ANGIE. Fencing.

ED. Even though I'm not sort of bright, like not at all actually, can't go on about ecology and that, conservation stuff, leave that to the experts –

He pulls a pocket-sized, well-thumbed copy of Greta Thunberg's No One Is Too Small to Make a Difference *from his coat –*

– leave that to Greta, she's got this – she really has got this, I think – thought I might be able to… Well. Sometimes you just need someone who can mend a fence. Hopefully, anyway.

ANGIE *smiles*.

ANGIE. I think so.

ED *crosses his fingers, pulls a face*.

A moment.

LAUREN. Right, Ed, think I've got…

She looks at her keys, and finds the right one.

I can just show you where you're staying.

No point waiting any longer for pasty-features.

DENNIS. I'm wolfing this so I can –

LAUREN. It's fine, Dad.

ANGIE *nods*.

Back in a bit.

ANGIE. In a bit then.

LAUREN. This way.

LAUREN *leaves*.

ED. Thanks for the, for these, Angie. And for letting me in and that.

I'll be back.

Not like Arnie, like *Terminator* sort of thing – 'I'll be back.' Have you seen it? *Terminator*? Just I'll be back to buy some cake and that. Vegan brownies. Tomorrow.

ANGIE. I'll make sure we've got some peppermint tea.

ED. Oh.

ED *leaves*.

A moment.

ANGIE. Nice lad.

DENNIS. Bit daft.

ANGIE *rolls her eyes*.

ANGIE. Best crack on.

ANGIE *carries on, emptying things from the cabinet into tins in the back room*.

DENNIS *has finished his pasty and beans*.

He brings his plate to the counter.

DENNIS. Angie?

ANGIE *reappears*.

ANGIE. All done?

DENNIS *nods*.

Just pop it there, love.

DENNIS. Right-o.

DENNIS *stands there*.

ANGIE. Anything else?

DENNIS. You're alright.

ANGIE *nods, and carries on clearing*.

Lots to do?

ANGIE. Bit.

ANGIE *ducks back into the kitchen*.

DENNIS *lingers a moment*.

He's thinking how to say something.

He nearly says it, then stops.

He just stands a minute, on his own.

ANGIE *is in the kitchen, washing up*.

He picks the poster up, takes it to the noticeboard.

Puts it up.

Looks at it a moment.

DENNIS. This competition looks good. Photography competition. For the birds.

A moment.

ANGIE (*off*). Oh right.

DENNIS. Thinking of giving it a go, actually.

The competition.

I'm getting quite into birdwatching, so...

Feels daft to have lived here all this time and not be, not know much about it.

Bit out of the loop with everyone. Like there's this whole world going on, right here, right here on my doorstep and I never really... But now...

Bit more time on my hands these days, I suppose.

Home-life's not as...

Dug out an old camera, anyway. It was...

Found it in the loft.

And I don't know much about the actual birds but I reckon I'll just pick it up, won't I?

ANGIE. Everyone'll help you, Kim and Phil or, you know. If you ask.

DENNIS. Yep. Yep.

A moment.

D'you think you'll have a go at it?

ANGIE (*off*). Me?

DENNIS. The competition, I mean.

ANGIE appears out of the kitchen, drying her hands on a tea towel.

She shakes her head.

ANGIE. Not for me all the... I'm more... just like seeing the birds really. And then they're gone.

DENNIS *nods*.

DENNIS. Right. Course.

A bit sadly.

Right.

ANGIE *goes back in the kitchen*.

A moment.

Thanks for the pasty, Angie. You have a good night.

He leaves.

2.

Sunday. Dusk.

LAUREN *is singing as she fetches the sign in. 'Texas Man' by The Chicks.*

ED *turns up.*

She spots him and stops singing. Tries to pretend that she wasn't just singing. He definitely heard her, but doesn't say anything.

LAUREN. Alright.

ED. Can I help?

LAUREN. I can manage.

ED. I know, obvs, I just… Might be a bit easier if we both…

LAUREN. Okay.

> ED *helps. It is a bit easier. They rest the sign against the inside wall.*

> Cheers.

> ED *makes a comedy muscle-flexing gesture.*

ED. Teamwork.

LAUREN *doesn't laugh.* ED *wishes he hadn't done it.*

He goes back outside the door again.

LAUREN. What are you doing?

ED. Oh I just –

ANGIE *spots* ED.

ANGIE. Hiya, love. Come on in.

ED. It's alright, you're shutting, I've left it, I'm late.

ANGIE. Just in time actually.

ED. You're clearing up.

ANGIE. We're not though. We're having a hoedown. Ish.

ED. Um.

LAUREN. Get in now.

ED *comes in.*

ANGIE *is grinning. She's holding out a guitar, for* LAUREN *to take.*

ED. What's...?

ANGIE. Tell him.

LAUREN *rolls her eyes.*

LAUREN. Neil, I think you'll have met him – grey hair, bright-blue scarf, for some reason my dad's taken against him –

ED. Yeah he did mention it actually.

LAUREN. Does this line-dancing night once a month in Ottringham. Normally they do it to a CD but Neil found out I play guitar, sing a bit, so he got me to go and do that for them. Last night.

ED. Sounds amazing.

LAUREN. It wasn't.

ED. Bet it was.

ANGIE. It was beautiful. You're your mum's daughter, for sure.

LAUREN *looks awkward*.

And I tell you what: line dancing's a blast. There's about four moves, you don't need a partner, just do it all in a big gang, it's lush.

ED. Feel like I missed out.

ANGIE. Well, you're in luck.

ED. What d'you mean?

ANGIE. I don't want to forget it all for next time – I've decided I'm going to make it my thing. Only went last night for Lauren really, moral support, but honestly, Ed, I loved it. So we're practising now, hopefully some of it'll get lodged in my head. Lauren agreed last night when she was flushed with success, I'm holding her to it. What?

ED. No it does sound lovely I just. Um. Don't know how?

ANGIE. Ed, I'll teach you. I've been once, I'm basically an expert.

LAUREN. It's only four moves.

ANGIE. And there's music.

ED. Really?

LAUREN *looks at* ED, *strums a chord*.

ANGIE. You'll pick it up no trouble.

ED *smiles*.

ED. I am actually quite excited about this.

ANGIE. All it is: it's just:

ANGIE *does a toe fan*.

That's called a toe fan. Fan your right toe out three times.

ED. Toe fan?

ANGIE. Yep.

ED. I might say 'tofu' instead. More vegan.

ED *does it*.

ANGIE. Right heel two times.

ED. Right two times.

ANGIE. Same back again.

ANGIE *does it.* ED *does it too.*

And then it's heel, toe, heel, toe, heel, toe, heel, toe.

ANGIE *does this.* ED *does it too.*

Step right, kick left, step left, right toe, and repeat.

They do.

Grapevine right. Scuff left. Grapevine left. Scuff right to turn.

They both do.

Step forward right, touch left. Step back, left together.

They both do.

You're a natural.

(*To* LAUREN.) He's good at this.

LAUREN *looks doubtful.*

ED. It does feel doable.

LAUREN. You ready?

ED. Might need reminding.

LAUREN. Ed, it's like four moves, just copy.

ED. Okay good plan.

LAUREN. There's a little introduction so, and then...

LAUREN *sings 'Texas Man' by The Chicks.*

She starts and then stops. ED *is looking at her in disbelief.*

What?

ED. You're an actual, real-life singer.

LAUREN *looks a bit embarrassed that he's noticed.* ANGIE *steps in.*

ANGIE. Ed.

ED. I mean that is… That is lovely.

ANGIE. Bit more dancing please.

ED. Soz.

ANGIE. Lauren?

LAUREN *starts the song again.*

ANGIE *and* ED *do some line dancing.*

ANGIE *is steady and good and enjoys it.*

ED *is chaotic but enthusiastic.*

He adds extra bits like whoops and a yeeha.

They are having a lovely time.

DENNIS *enters, with a camera, scruffy birding coat, bits of greenery attached.*

They notice him.

They stop.

LAUREN. Sorry, Dad.

She puts the guitar down.

DENNIS. No it's, um…

DENNIS *is a bit winded. He recovers though (or tries to).*

Evening.

LAUREN *and* ANGIE *share a look.*

I didn't mean to… I'm interrupting.

DENNIS *looks at* LAUREN*'s guitar.* LAUREN *is not sure what to do.*

Sorry. I'll go.

ANGIE *steps in.*

ANGIE. You're fine, Dennis. What can I get you? Pasty and beans?

DENNIS. No, no, it's, um…

DENNIS looks at his watch, turns to go.

LAUREN. We were just line dancing, Dad. We had a go yesterday at Neil's line-dancing night. In Ottringham. So we just thought we'd go through it again now, keep it all, keep it fresh. Didn't mean to…

ANGIE holds a plate out to him.

ANGIE. Here. You'll be helping me out.

DENNIS takes it.

DENNIS (*quietly*). Cheers.

He goes to sit down.

ANGIE. Alright if we come join you?

DENNIS. Oh.

This isn't exactly a yes, but they join him anyway.

ANGIE brings round three vegan brownies, a pot of tea for two and a peppermint tea.

ANGIE. Right, gang, we're celebrating.

ED. Celebrating…?

ANGIE. Last day open. For the year. We flipping did it.

ANGIE high-fives LAUREN.

LAUREN. Just.

ANGIE. Out with a bang.

DENNIS. Busy one, was it?

ANGIE. Bit.

DENNIS. They've ringed a couple of long-eared owls at the obs. That'll be what's brought everyone in.

ED. And that white-tailed eagle. Oh my days.

LAUREN. Don't start.

ED. It was: amazing.

LAUREN. We know. No one's shut up about it all day.

ED. Oh.

LAUREN. Even Angie.

ED. Did you see it?

ANGIE. Lauren held the fort while Neil and me nipped to the wetlands. Only caught a glimpse as it was flying over but. Pretty special.

LAUREN. Here we go.

ED. Wasn't it though? All big and like, majestic. Eagle-y. Never thought I'd see a real-life white-tailed eagle. In East Yorkshire. On a Sunday.

ANGIE. Somehow it took me by surprise that it actually had a white tail.

LAUREN. Please tell me you got a picture, Dad?

DENNIS. Eh?

LAUREN. Reckon this photography prize has sent people a bit, you know. And mostly I was just like: I've given you your teacake please stop talking to me but actually, in fairness, some of the photos they've taken are pretty impressive. Neil's – you could pick out individual feathers.

DENNIS. Course you could.

LAUREN. Been crossing my fingers you've got a good one and all.

DENNIS *nods*.

DENNIS. Oh. Loads, I reckon. Yeah. Loads.

LAUREN *looks doubtful*.

LAUREN. Really?

DENNIS *nods*.

DENNIS. Course.

LAUREN (*carefully*). That's good then.

DENNIS. Flew over Canal Scrape when I was there so...

ED. No way! Me too. I didn't see you, Dennis. I'd've said hello.

DENNIS *gestures towards the bits of undergrowth he's stuck in his clothes.*

DENNIS. Camouflage.

ED. Can we see your photos?

DENNIS. Take a while. Still got to get the film developed.

ED. Oh.

DENNIS. Proper camera this. Not keen on these digital ones. Too fussy.

LAUREN. Also, quite expensive.

DENNIS. This does me alright. Them others, they're a bit 'all the gear and no idea'.

LAUREN. D'you mean Neil?

DENNIS. Just mean anyone who moves here, does a bit of birding, thinks they know everything just cos they've got a fancy camera. Tripod. Scarf.

LAUREN. So Neil then.

DENNIS. Means it'll be extra-special when I get myself this prize.

Two fingers up to the bloody, newcomers, hobbyists, and a proper well done to the people who've committed to it.

LAUREN. You started yesterday.

DENNIS. But I've lived here all my life.

LAUREN. Never been that interested in birds though. Or taken any photographs. I'm pretty sure you're fibbing about the ones you took today.

DENNIS *looks very cross.*

ANGIE. When's it all over?

DENNIS. What?

ANGIE. Sick of this prize already, it's been two days.

LAUREN. Closing date's not till spring. So, you know: strap in.

ANGIE. Seems like a very long time to be this competitive.

DENNIS. It's exactly the right amount of time, Angie. Makes perfect sense when you think about it.

LAUREN *sighs, rolls her eyes.*

You get the chance to photograph the birds flying south in the autumn, snap snap snap. Get the chance to look at the ones who've stayed for the winter, which are just as interesting, actually. Probably. Then there's a last-minute chance to get a photograph of everything arriving back in the spring. Very well thought-through.

DENNIS *notices they're all looking at him.*

What?

LAUREN. We understand the concept of migration, Dad. You're birdsplaining.

ANGIE. You are a bit.

DENNIS. I don't see what you two have against a very straightforward photography competition.

LAUREN. Just another chance for birdwatchers to be weird, isn't it? Don't really think they needed one.

ED. Do you not like them then?

LAUREN. No.

DENNIS. You like Angie.

LAUREN. Angie's not a dickhead about it. She just likes sort of seeing the birds.

ANGIE. I do.

LAUREN. Which I get. Sort of. The rest though: all this being like obsessed with, I dunno, telescopes, cameras, competitions, seeing stuff first, rare stuff, before everyone

else sees it, or before it dies cos it's been blown off-course
by a gale or something, which no one seems to think is sad.

ANGIE. I do.

LAUREN. All just weird, isn't it? Lonely, middle-aged men
with cameras being weird. And Angie.

ANGIE. I don't have a camera.

LAUREN. Maybe that's why you're alright.

DENNIS. Maybe that's why no one believes her when she
claims she's seen stuff.

ANGIE. Here we go.

LAUREN. Don't, Dad.

ED. I don't…

    ANGIE *rolls her eyes.*

ANGIE. Doesn't matter.

    ED *looks confused.*

LAUREN. Years and years ago, Angie saw a thingy, albatross.

ED. No. Way. Really?

    ANGIE *looks at* ED, *shrugs a bit, nods.* ED *is amazed.*

They are like the Brad Pitt of seabirds.

LAUREN. And then the other birders – mostly, it has to be said,
men – just decided she couldn't've done, cos they're really,
properly rare round here, albatrosses, like one every few
decades, if you're lucky. So if anyone was off to see one, it
should be someone with like, a massive telescope or
whatever. They reckoned. Should've been one of them. So at
first they tried to explain other things it probably was, and
Angie was just like 'it was an albatross' –

ANGIE. It was.

LAUREN. And then some of them, the dickheads really,
decided she was making it up, turned it into like a running
joke.

ED. Oh.

ANGIE. On the plus side: I got to see an albatross.

ED. What was it like?

ANGIE *thinks*.

ANGIE. Big?

ANGIE *shrugs*.

And, er. Well. Beautiful.

LAUREN. Till everyone was a dickhead about it.

ANGIE. Didn't matter.

DENNIS. Should've taken a photo.

ANGIE. I'd rather just enjoy it happening, Dennis. Just do that. The important stuff stays with you anyway, I think. Keep it with you, remember how it felt. The rest...

A moment.

ED. Can I just say: that is exactly what this weekend has been like for me.

No albatrosses but. Obvs but.

And it probably sounds daft or whatever, out loud, and the interview tomorrow, that might swing things in the other direction but, I do think sometimes it's worth just saying the daft stuff out loud – isn't it though?

LAUREN. Not in your interview.

ED. Cos literally, everyone I've met has been like decent and interesting, showed me round or helped me out or, I dunno. Met all of you which just feels sort of... Dennis has made me feel properly welcome at his. My own mug.

DENNIS *looks embarrassed*.

Plus I'm not being funny, Angie, but these brownies, vegan brownies, from nowhere. They are the best thing I've ever eaten in my whole entire life.

ANGIE. There's more if you...

ED. Peppermint tea as well. Specially.

ANGIE. Cross we'd run out yesterday.

ED. And then just, this place. Like I'm used to birdwatching
with my grandad back home – Dudley, Wolverhampton,
anywhere with a canal. He goes fishing, I tag along with a
flask and some binoculars. Which is, you know: good. But
here's just, I dunno. The sand and, and the sea, waves
crashing, ships passing, wind blowing foam along the beach,
or ripples in the grass, like material but. Softer, dunno. And
like I know it's on the edge of things, and you do, you feel
that too – must be a nightmare when you run out of loo roll
or, yeah, winter, but. Mostly, it does feel a bit sort of magic.
Just does.

LAUREN. Maybe do say that in your interview actually, it's
quite good.

ED. I can't tell if you're taking the piss out of me.

LAUREN. Nope.

ED. Oh.

ED *smiles.*

LAUREN. Pretty much everything else I've said to you has
been though, just FYI. And I can't see that changing in the
future.

ED. Good to know.

LAUREN *and* ED *smile at each other.*

DENNIS *changes the subject.*

DENNIS. Didn't realise you were shutting up today.

ANGIE. Just till spring. While it's quiet.

DENNIS. Course.

ANGIE. So you'll be pasty-less till Easter.

DENNIS. I'll manage.

ANGIE. Will you?

DENNIS. Course.

ANGIE. Lauren's a bit worried since she moved out you've not been –

LAUREN. Angie.

DENNIS. It's been four days. She's fussing.

ANGIE. Said something quite dangerous happened with a microwave shepherd's pie.

LAUREN. Wasn't a microwave one, it was in a foil tray.

DENNIS. Lauren.

ANGIE. Oh.

DENNIS. Lesson learnt.

ANGIE. Thing is: I do think you rely on this place a bit. And we're open again next spring, till October time but then we're sort of, well. Done.

DENNIS. What d'you mean?

ANGIE. They've got a new café all planned in the Discovery Centre, they'll have that open instead. Said did I want to try running it but to be honest, think I'd rather free myself up a bit. Reckon I can manage just selling jams and pickles at craft fairs and that. Farmers markets. Like a little business. And then… who knows? New adventures, a bit. Hopefully.

Thinking of calling it: Angie's Jams.

Neil said keep it simple. Easy to remember; easy to fit on the labels.

DENNIS. Right.

ANGIE. The new place'll have one of those proper coffee machines anyway. All lattes and that. Macchiatos. Too much spelling.

DENNIS. So this place'll just…

ANGIE *shrugs*.

ANGIE. But, I was wondering if it might be useful to do you a bit of a crash course, cooking-wise? Nothing fancy just, heating things up, to begin with, then you could get the hang of making a nice sausage casserole maybe, poaching an egg. Veggies.

DENNIS *frowns*.

DENNIS. You're alright.

ANGIE. It's no bother.

DENNIS. Yeah but –

ANGIE. I'm quite good at meals for one. Lot of practice.

DENNIS. Don't need teaching how to poach a bloody egg.

ANGIE. Oh.

LAUREN. Are you sure?

DENNIS. Yes I'm sure.

ANGIE. Course. Sorry. Didn't mean to… I wasn't… Sorry.

A moment.

Be busy with your photographs too, of course.

DENNIS *nods*.

Not many things to see in winter but.

A moment.

DENNIS. Well. Best be off.

Thanks, Angie. You two.

DENNIS *leaves*.

ED *downs his drink too. It is still a bit hot.*

ANGIE. You alright, love?

ED. Yeah, um, I just, I better go as well really. Start getting ready. For tomorrow. Big day and that. Big interview.

ANGIE. Hope it goes well.

ED. Me too.

ANGIE. I'm sure it'll be fine.

ED. Thanks for my brownie, my peppermint tea. And just: all this, really.

ANGIE. Any time.

ANGIE *can see* ED *doesn't want to leave. He's looking at* LAUREN, *a bit shy.*

Better go start this washing up.

She goes into the kitchen.

A moment.

LAUREN. See you then.

ED. Oh. Yeah.

Or, hopefully I mean. If I get this job and. I dunno.

LAUREN. You will do.

ED *crosses his fingers, goofily.*

LAUREN *raises her eyebrows.*

ED *uncrosses his fingers, wishes he hadn't done it.*

ED. I have got an idea actually. A thing to suggest sort of, in the interview.

LAUREN. Oh right.

ED. Yeah. Cos like this afternoon, when the white-tailed eagle was about, I was just like lucky, really, that I was in the right place, right time. Just sort of followed some people, tagged along a bit. And they were well nice and everything, so welcoming, but if I was less sort of, like, less up for joining in I guess, asking for help or whatever, more sort of, I dunno, shy or, I wouldn't've known about it, wouldn't've had a way of knowing about it. So I thought: maybe, there could be like, just really simple but, probably stupid actually but, just like an information board. Like maybe here or something. 'Recent Sightings.' So people could, if they didn't know who to ask, or just didn't like asking, they could find out what to look out for, if there's anything special about or…

ED *notices* LAUREN *is pulling a face.*

You think it's a rubbish idea. Fair enough. Glad I tested it out.

LAUREN. No, I just…

LAUREN *goes over to the board, takes down a few papers. Underneath it says 'Recent Sightings'.*

ED. Oh.

ED *is a bit deflated.*

LAUREN. No one's filled it in for ages though. You could say you'd fill it in.

ED. Yeah. Yeah. Good idea.

He's quite sad.

LAUREN. Well, I better…

ED. Course. See you then.

LAUREN. See you.

ED. Um.

ED *looks a bit uncertain.*

LAUREN. What's up?

ED *makes a decision.*

ED. Just, feel like I need to say: that singing, before, it was really like, I dunno. It really did sound lovely.

LAUREN *rolls her eyes.*

LAUREN. Right.

ED. Did.

LAUREN. My mum sounded lovely. I'm just okay.

But that's fine, I mean. Still like playing and that. Makes me feel a bit closer to her or something.

It was her guitar, so… That's why, um. Angie said I could keep it here, so I can practise in the quiet times. She can listen. It was at my dad's so… Think he gets a bit sad still, hearing it.

Our place is – his place now – it's quite quiet.

ED. Did your mum, um. Did she die?

LAUREN *nods*.

LAUREN. Yeah. Few years ago but. Yeah.

ED. Mine too.

LAUREN *looks at* ED.

A moment.

Must miss her.

LAUREN*, nearly imperceptibly, nods*.

Miss mine all the time. Doesn't go away, does it?

A moment.

She'd think it was well stupid I've gone vegan but I just think on this one probably Greta knows best.

LAUREN *thinks*.

LAUREN. Maybe.

They both smile.

ED. Anyway, I better…

LAUREN. See you then.

She goes into the kitchen.

ED *looks disappointed.*

Does a gesture to himself, like he's saying 'Ed, you idiot.'

He's done this quite a lot.

LAUREN (*still in the kitchen*). Ed?

ED. Yeah?

ED*'s heart lifts.*

LAUREN *appears with some bin bags.*

LAUREN. Couldn't drop these round the back, could you? Just in the big wheelie bin.

ED*'s heart sinks.*

ED. Oh. Um. Course.

ED *takes the bags.*

LAUREN. Also…

ED *looks up.*

LAUREN *kisses* ED.

Hope tomorrow goes well. Obvs. Come back and see us soon?

ED *blinks.*

He picks up the bin bags, smiles at LAUREN, *leaves.*

Spring

3.

Saturday evening.

ED *has taken the leaflets off the 'Recent Sightings' board, and filled it in.*

It says:

'REED BUNTING
LITTLE STINT
PLENTY OF SWIFTS (BUT NOT TAYLOR)'

ED *carries the sign in from outside.*

He sits down by the sign, empties his pockets and his bag: a pencil, two wheels, some screws, a drill, a screwdriver.

He draws crosses where he needs to drill on two of the sign's legs.

He checks to see no one's watching.

He goes for it.

LAUREN *and* ANGIE *appear in the kitchen doorway.*

LAUREN. What the –

ED. I know.

LAUREN. What are you doing?

ED. I'm putting: wheels, on the sign.

Hope that's alright, Angie.

ANGIE. Oh. Course. I mean. Um.

LAUREN *gives* ANGIE *a look.*

I'll leave you two to chat.

ANGIE *goes back through to the kitchen.*

ED. Was hoping it'd be a surprise but I didn't think through the drill. Like it's hard to be subtle with:

ED *drills the air for a second.*

Isn't it? Not to worry.

D'you not think it's a good plan? I think it's a really good plan. Cos what you'll be able to do, you'll be able to just tip it onto the wheels like:

ED *tips the sandwich board up onto the two legs he's marked out for wheels.*

Wheel it round, no probs. Into the café, out of the café. Wheel it off into the sunset if you like.

LAUREN. Why would I do that?

ED *doesn't know.*

A moment.

ED. You seem quite cross.

LAUREN. Cos I'm absolutely fine with carrying the sign.

ED. Just thought, I dunno. This is something I can actually help with, isn't it?

LAUREN. Have I asked you to help?

ED. No but –

LAUREN. Well I don't need your help then.

If I was struggling, I'd just ask Angie to do it.

ED. Now you won't have to.

LAUREN *gives* ED *a look.*

What?

LAUREN *shrugs, sighs.*

Just want to feel like I'm doing something.

LAUREN. You're doing plenty.

ED. Not as much as you.

LAUREN. That would be impossible in terms of biology.

Doing enough alright? We're managing.

ED. Don't want you to feel like you're by yourself.

LAUREN. I don't.

ED. Yeah, but –

LAUREN. If anything…

ED. What?

LAUREN. Doesn't matter. Come here.

LAUREN *hugs* ED. *Then holds his shoulders, speaks to him slowly.*

I sort of need you to chill, the fuck, out.

Alright?

ED *doesn't know what to say.*

Ed?

ED *smiles.*

ED. Do my best.

LAUREN. Stuff's gone fast – you getting this job, us, moving in together, et cetera –

ED. Quite a big et cetera. Or, you know, it will be.

LAUREN. We'll figure it all out. Don't have to start doing everything for me, just cos –

ED. It was just while I had all the tools and that. We were, me and Phil, building a fence all day, round the dune where, round all the nests, little terns. Just FYI, a really good fence. Electric to keep the foxes out, wood to keep everything else out, very neat corners. My second proudest Tern Warden moment so far.

LAUREN. What's your first?

ED. Oh, um.

He grins, nods towards the 'Recent Sightings' board.

LAUREN *looks.*

LAUREN (*unimpressed*). 'Plenty of Swifts'.

ED (*as if it is the best joke in the world*). 'But Not Taylor'.

LAUREN. Ed, that is a terrible, terrible joke.

ED. Some would say: a 'dad' joke. (Just practising.)

And I thought, while everything was handy, the tools and that, I could sort this.

LAUREN. Ed, the sign is: tip of the iceberg. Isn't it though? There's all the cleaning, cooking –

ED. Did you not like the vegan pizzas?

LAUREN. Not really, if I'm honest.

ED. Okay.

LAUREN. It was a flatbread with some tomato on. It was essentially damp pitta.

ED. I'll get better.

And, well. I'll leave this.

ED *starts to pack his stuff away.*

LAUREN *looks at the sign for a moment.*

LAUREN. In fairness, putting wheels on the sign is probably a good plan.

ED *looks at* LAUREN.

What?

ED. Nothing.

LAUREN. What?

ED *starts getting on with the sign again.*

I'm allowed to change my mind.

ED. Yep.

LAUREN. Not about vegan pizza though. That was rank.

ED *nods*.

ED (*a little sadly*). Yep.

LAUREN *breathes out*.

LAUREN. I'm being a knob.

ED *nods, smiles*.

ED. We both are. That's why it works.

LAUREN *kisses* ED.

D'you know what I think would be nice? A little walk, after you're done here. Like a nice romantic walk, just the two of us, down Beacon Lane, we can watch the sunset, I can show you my new fence.

LAUREN. Right.

ED. What?

LAUREN. Ed, that could not sound less romantic.

ED. I sort of have to though.

LAUREN. Why?

ED. Neil's lent me his camera, it's well snazzy.

LAUREN. Why?

ED. Cos he's got all his photographs entered already. For the prize.

LAUREN. Yeah but why's he lent it – ?

ED. Oh, so I can take some photos. Of my fence.

A moment.

LAUREN. You are kidding.

ED. I'm proud of it. If I get some really nice photos of it now while it's all neat I can like show people next time I'm looking for a job. Cos it just, it is good. Think we did a good job and that. And I know, from the outside, probably seems daft we put all this time and energy into looking after these, well, these like silly little birds but they're actually, they're well important. To me and... I dunno. Everyone really.

And when you can spend the afternoon, when you spend the afternoon just quiet, just sat in the hide or whatever, on your own, just watching them. And they seem happy. Seem at home. And you just get to think: I did that. It's a bit of. Sort of. Yeah. Bit magic.

Might tweet Greta. She'll be well impressed.

LAUREN (*to the kitchen*). Angie.

ANGIE *appears*.

ANGIE. What's up, love?

LAUREN. Did you hear that? Ed wants us to go for a walk together down Beacon Lane, a romantic walk, so we can take some really nice photos of his fence.

ANGIE. Oh.

LAUREN. That is the man I love. Who I've literally made another human with.

ED. Lauren.

ED *looks wide-eyed*.

LAUREN. Oh, Angie knows.

ED. What?

ANGIE. Congratulations, love.

ED. Oh.

Cheers, Angie. We're delighted.

Thought we weren't telling anyone.

LAUREN. We're not, I just spent most of this morning vomming, Angie figured it out.

ED. Sorry. Was it grim?

LAUREN. I'd say it was sort of a bonding experience, wasn't it?

ANGIE *smiles*.

ANGIE. I do think, if I know now, it'd be a good idea to tell your dad sooner rather than later. Just so he's got time to take it all in.

LAUREN. It's actually none of his business, is the thing. Like, we're adults, we're good people, we've got this.

ANGIE. Be nice to include him though. In the good news.

ED *and* LAUREN *look at each other*.

ED. Tonight?

LAUREN. Tonight.

ANGIE. Good cos, um…

DENNIS *arrives*.

DENNIS. Evening.

He's had a bad day.

ANGIE. Everything alright?

DENNIS. Not really.

He sits down, a bit defeated.

LAUREN *gives* ED *a look, shakes her head, as if to say 'not tonight'.*

LAUREN. What's happened? Dad.

DENNIS *takes a pack of photographs out of his pocket, drops them on the table.*

LAUREN *looks at them.*

LAUREN. Oh. Shit.

DENNIS. Three films' worth. Must be something up with it. The camera.

LAUREN. Are you sure you haven't just – ?

DENNIS. Sod off. Not something I've done, it's this. Got damp or, damaged. Something.

LAUREN *shows* ANGIE *and* ED *a photograph. It is just
black and brown and blurry, with a sticker on saying that the
film was damaged.*

The whole lot.

ANGIE *pulls a face.*

And I wouldn't mind but I have been absolutely banging on
to everyone, anyone who'll listen for, what is it, six, seven
months now? About how much better it is to use a real
camera, use real film, take a bit of time with it. Which, I'm
not sure if it's even true, just read it somewhere. The
internet. Thought it made me sound like I knew what I was
on about. Thought it'd sound impressive, they'd take me a
bit more...

Been so careful when to take a picture. Cos you've got to – I
read about it, you don't want to... If you're pinning down a
moment, forever – which is what a photo is, isn't it, really –
you want it to be the best moment. That's the thing to catch.
Just wanted to show them... I dunno. Might not see
everything they see, might not get to hear about it, cos they
don't tell me, do they? Not in the loop. Very much out of the
loop, actually, as it goes. But I can spot something myself,
when it's there, take a decent... And then maybe I'd just...

No one can argue with that, can they? Anyone questions you,
just show them that.

But: no.

LAUREN. Dad.

DENNIS. So, I've had quite a shitty day.

ANGIE. Here.

She hands him a plate with a pasty and beans.

DENNIS. Cheers, Angie. One good thing.

ANGIE. It'll be alright, love.

DENNIS. Bloody won't.

LAUREN *has an idea.*

LAUREN. If we could get hold of a digital camera for you –

DENNIS. Got to be all handed in tomorrow, love.

LAUREN. Yeah I know you've waited till the last possible minute to get your photos developed, which is both annoying and typical.

DENNIS. I didn't know, did I?

LAUREN. But if we could do it now, so you got all day birding and, just in case, you could email in your best shot as a competition entry, before midnight, would you do it? We'd help with the emailing bit.

DENNIS. I know how to bloody email.

LAUREN. But would you?

DENNIS *thinks*.

DENNIS. Maybe.

LAUREN. Ed…

ED. Oh, um.

ED *gets a very fancy-looking digital camera out of his bag.*

He hangs on to it.

It's a lot easier to use than it looks. Like I just had a couple of goes, got the hang of it straight away, so that's not a biggie.

ED *looks at* LAUREN. *She nods.*

Here.

He holds it out to DENNIS.

DENNIS. Who's lent you this?

ED *and* LAUREN *share a look.*

ED. Um.

LAUREN. Neil.

DENNIS. Oh for –

LAUREN. He's got his photos sent in, so he was just like: of course, borrow it. Ed wanted to take some photos of his new fence he's put up, round the little terns, where their nests are, keep them safe, protect the little terns. He's very proud of it. I know.

ED. It is literally my job.

LAUREN. But he can do that tomorrow.

Borrow it now, you've still time to get a photo in. Fingers crossed for a few decent birds in the morning. What d'you reckon? Plan? Course it is. Just need one bit of luck, one good bird, bit of time to get the right shot, it's yours for the taking. You can do it still. You can.

DENNIS *takes the camera.*

Turns it around a bit. Has a good look.

DENNIS. Right. Well. Okay.

LAUREN. You've got this.

In the meantime: Dad, can I borrow your van? Me and Ed need to nip to Aldi, go get some ingredients for tomorrow nights' stew. You're invited by the way. We were off to do it tonight but this way there's more time, for stewing. We can look at your photos and all. Cos you'll have taken them. By tomorrow.

DENNIS. Oh.

DENNIS *passes* LAUREN *the car keys.*

LAUREN. Alright to nip off a bit early, Angie?

ANGIE. Course.

LAUREN *smiles.*

LAUREN. See you at ours tomorrow then, Dad? Seven-ish?

Ed.

ED. Oh.

LAUREN *leaves.*

See you both.

ED *leaves*.

DENNIS *looks at the camera a minute, uncertain*.

ANGIE. Neil is actually, very nice.

DENNIS. Course he is.

ANGIE. He actually is.

DENNIS. No one's got a bad word to say about him. With his bloody, line dancing –

ANGIE. The line dancing's fun.

DENNIS. So Lauren tells me. Says she's singing there once a month. And his birdwatching –

ANGIE. You love birdwatching.

DENNIS. I grew up with it, Angie.

ANGIE. Not really.

DENNIS. It's in my bones.

ANGIE. Is it?

DENNIS. Course it is.

ANGIE. If you say so.

DENNIS. And I tell you what: it's more than a three-grand camera and a North Face.

ANGIE. Dennis.

DENNIS. It is. He's an accountant who took early retirement and he always will be. And he's boring. And he's from Leeds.

ANGIE. I don't see what you've got against Neil, Dennis.

He's just…

DENNIS. Nice?

ANGIE. Are you jealous, Dennis? Is that what this is?

DENNIS. Hardly.

ANGIE *smiles*.

ANGIE. You do realise – and I don't know why I'm telling you this, it is absolutely none of your business but, you do realise, Neil's…

ANGIE *doesn't finish*.

DENNIS. A twat?

ANGIE. No, Dennis. He's, well, he's gay.

DENNIS *didn't realise*.

And he's my friend. And the thing is: I don't have that many friends, actually. I don't have a lot of people in my life who are just nice to me. I had Victoria. And we'd been through stuff. Together. And she could be relied on to be there for me. And she could be relied on to take the piss.

DENNIS. She did take the piss a lot.

ANGIE. Now she's gone.

And Neil's different, obviously. But he's decent and funny and normal, bit strange sometimes, in a good way and, I dunno. Nice? Think he probably thinks the same about me. That is being friends, I think. But I don't have many so. Might be wrong.

A moment.

Better do some washing up.

ANGIE *goes into the kitchen*.

DENNIS *looks like he is thinking: 'shit'*.

He listens to ANGIE *for a minute. She is washing up crossly, clanking plates in the kitchen*.

DENNIS *doesn't know what to say*.

DENNIS. Angie?

Plates clatter.

I'm sorry, Angie. I don't know what I was saying really but. Anyway.

ANGIE (*off*). It's fine.

It isn't.

DENNIS. Will you come out here so I can say sorry properly? Please. To your face.

A moment.

ANGIE *comes out of the kitchen, wiping her hands on a tea towel.*

ANGIE. Go on then.

DENNIS. Feel like a bit of a prick.

ANGIE. A bit?

DENNIS. Well. I am. Sorry.

A moment.

ANGIE (*downbeat*). It's alright.

DENNIS. Doesn't sound it.

ANGIE *smiles, shakes her head.*

ANGIE. Leave it, Dennis.

DENNIS. Just want to know you're alright.

ANGIE. Well I'm not to be honest.

ANGIE *stops, takes a deep breath, settles herself.*

Sorry, didn't mean to snap, it's just... Well.

My Jenny's anniversary. Today so. Not at my best.

A moment.

DENNIS. Oh.

I didn't...

ANGIE. Always hard so. Usually just keep to myself. Light a candle. Whatever that does. Let myself be sad, just for... Well.

And I managed all day alright but, just but, there's a lot going on, isn't there? Babies everywhere. Cos it's spring I suppose. Everything's…

She'd've been twenty this year. Feels, I don't know. Meaningful, somehow. Don't know why.

A moment.

DENNIS *smiles at* ANGIE.

DENNIS. You'd've been such a lovely mum, Angie.

ANGIE *frowns.*

You would.

ANGIE *sighs.*

ANGIE. The thing is, Dennis: I am a mum. Doesn't stop just cos… Still going. Like breathing. Bit more… Think about her, miss her all the time. Still a tight little knot in my… Just here, just by my…

ANGIE *holds her hand up to her heart.*

Look at Lauren sometimes and I think: you should've had a boat mate. There should've been two of you figuring all this out. Might've made it all a bit… I don't know.

It is such a lonely thing, to lose a child. Maybe the loneliest thing.

And then her dad sort of… Don't blame him. I mean I wouldn't try and outrun it, I don't think you can, but… We were, properly young.

And I had Victoria to lean on.

And I did.

Never seemed to mind.

DENNIS. Course she didn't.

ANGIE. People say to me all the time, people who don't know: did you never fancy having kids? You'd have been a lovely mum, Angie. And I have to just, bite my tongue. Save them feeling bad, being uncomfortable. Can't say, not even quietly: I am a mum. Cos...

But you should know, Dennis. You should know not to say it.

DENNIS *is quiet.*

DENNIS. I'm sorry, Angie.

ANGIE *shrugs.*

A moment.

He opens his mouth to say something, but thinks better of it.

ANGIE *looks at* DENNIS.

ANGIE. What?

DENNIS. Doesn't matter.

He looks at the camera. Picks it up. Leaves.

ANGIE *sits for a moment, just by herself.*

4.

Sunday evening.

The 'Recent Sightings' board is filled in:

'DUNLIN
LITTLE GREBE
GREYLAG GOOSE'

LAUREN *wheels the sign in.*

ANGIE *watches, smiling.*

LAUREN. Yeah I know.

LAUREN *smiles.*

I mean he does my head in most of the time but.

ANGIE. Swoon.

LAUREN. Sorted everything for tonight. Like he's making this lovely lentil and mushroom stew that he makes, from scratch, it's really nice, and we've told my dad it's shepherd's pie, not mentioned the V-word, so he's not on edge about it. Reckon then we can all have a sort of upbeat, calm chat, explain about, explain like he's off to be a grandad – which obviously is quite a lot to get your head round, quite a big thing in your mid-forties, fingers crossed we'll just skip over that, no biggie – show him the scan and that.

ANGIE. Spot on.

LAUREN *looks at* ANGIE *a moment.*

LAUREN. You alright?

ANGIE. Oh, um.

LAUREN. Like I absolutely didn't mean for you to find out how you did, with me throwing up and that. That wasn't the plan. I mean vomming's never the plan but...

ANGIE. It's not that, love. It's...

A moment.

Well.

A moment.

Oh, just. It's brilliant news, it is, and you and Ed'll be just... That's the thing.

And then it's, there's some little sad bits too, and they're just mine, I just, I have to sort of...

But you and Ed...

ED *arrives.*

ED. Think I might need to call tonight off.

LAUREN. We've been through this, it'll be fine, be better once it's done.

ED. No I don't mean, not worried about, I mean I want it to, to go well, definitely but, don't want to hurt anyone's feelings, obvs –

LAUREN. Good start.

ED. Thing is: I'm in trouble.

LAUREN. What d'you mean?

ED. Work stuff. They've called me into the office. Now.

LAUREN. Phil has?

ED *nods*.

ED. On a Sunday.

LAUREN. What's he doing in the office on a Sunday?

ED. Well I think probably technically it's an emergency.
Conservation-wise. And I think probably, technically, it's my
fault.

ANGIE. D'you want to sit down, love?

ED. Better not, Angie. Better go really. Go get sacked.

LAUREN. You won't get sacked.

ED. I've properly messed up.

LAUREN. How?

ED. Yesterday we put the fence up, round the little terns' nests.
Cos it's quite hard to tell they're nests really – just little scrapes
of sand, shallow, hard to see, and the eggs are all camouflaged
to look like pebbles, so I thought like: what would Greta do?
She'd put a fence up, wouldn't she? Protect them.

LAUREN. That's good, Ed. That's your job.

ED. Yeah but then today, this morning I think, someone's
climbed over, trampled everywhere, with their big massive
boots. Everywhere just, footprints. Cos of me.

LAUREN. How is that cos of you?

ED. Cos I put the fence up. And a sign that said 'Little tern
nesting ground: please keep out'. So they knew where it was.
That was my idea – the sign. Thought people would be extra-
careful if they knew there was something rare, something
fragile nesting there. Honestly I'm such a moron.

LAUREN. Ed, you're not a moron.

ED. Like the polar ice caps are melting, water levels rising, there's all this plastic in the ocean – I've got a keep cup, it's nothing, it's not enough. Is it though? They're destroying acres and acres of orangutans' natural habitat every day. For palm oil. Which is just... Feels like there's not much I can do about any of that. But I can help keep some little terns safe, I thought. Just while they have their chicks.

Apparently not. Apparently, the opposite. Apparently if you put a fence round something and a sign explaining why it's precious, people see that as quite a good reason to trample over it.

Now I'm summoned to this emergency meeting. Not even started the stew.

LAUREN *hugs* ED.

LAUREN. Deep breaths.

ED *takes some deep breaths*.

Don't worry about the stew.

I'll explain to my dad, we'll do it another night when stuff's calmer. It'll all be fine.

ANGIE. It will be alright, love.

ED. Better go.

ED *leaves*.

LAUREN *looks at* ANGIE.

LAUREN. Won't be alright, will it?

ANGIE. Might be.

The thing about Ed: he's a worrier.

LAUREN *sighs, goes through to the kitchen*.

DENNIS *enters*.

ANGIE. Hello, Dennis.

DENNIS. Ed alright?

ANGIE. Having a bit of a day. Thinks he's in trouble cos of the fence he put up. And the sign.

DENNIS. Oh.

ANGIE. But I'm sure it's not as bad as he thinks.

DENNIS. I wanted to say, Angie: I'm sorry for, for putting my foot in it yesterday.

ANGIE. It's alright.

DENNIS. I know I put my foot in it sometimes.

ANGIE. Some days are just bad days.

DENNIS *doesn't know what to say.*

How's things with you anyway? Got your photos in?

DENNIS. Well, they're not in yet, but I do think I've got a few nice ones. Think you'll like them, anyway.

ANGIE. Oh.

DENNIS. D'you want to…?

ANGIE *nods.* DENNIS *gets his camera out.*

He presses some buttons.

Might take a minute to…

ANGIE *looks at the camera screen.*

These first ones are just me getting the hang of… Some blurry ones of oystercatchers. Herring gulls, herring gulls, thought it was a moth, it was actually a pebble, but then…

ANGIE *peers closely.*

ANGIE. Wow.

DENNIS. Nesting. I mean: there's eggs and that. Underneath. Can't see them. It's sat on them.

What d'you reckon?

(*Shouting through to the kitchen.*) Lauren, love, come and look at these photos.

(*To* ANGIE.) Got to be a prizewinner, hasn't it? That much detail. No one else'll... Got to be.

LAUREN *comes out of the kitchen to look at the camera screen.*

She's less impressed.

LAUREN. What is it?

DENNIS. Well. Probably doesn't look much but think it's – I mean I don't know do I, still learning – but I think it's quite rare.

LAUREN. It's quite surprised.

ANGIE. What d'you mean?

DENNIS. Protected, aren't they? The, thingy, species. Little terns. Don't normally get to see them up close like this. On their eggs.

LAUREN *and* ANGIE *exchange a look.*

What?

LAUREN. Was it you?

DENNIS. What d'you mean?

LAUREN. Someone's climbed over the new fence Ed's put up, trampled over all the sand dunes, churned everything up – nests, eggs – disturbed everything. Like a dickhead.

DENNIS. I mean I might've nipped over the fence, just quickly but –

LAUREN. Footprints everywhere, Ed says. All the bits they're trying to keep safe, someone's trampled, basically stamped on half the nests.

A moment.

DENNIS (*quietly*). Shit.

LAUREN. Really?

DENNIS. I kept a, a good distance.

LAUREN. These look pretty close up.

DENNIS. There's a zoom.

A moment.

Being honest: I am a bit worried it was me.

LAUREN. No shit, Dad.

DENNIS. The idea sort of came to me this morning and I did, I did hop over the fence and –

LAUREN. So they're your footprints. You're the reason Ed's getting bollocked. That's your fault. Trampled the nests, probably broken the eggs. Somehow managed, in a couple of minutes, to bugger up an entire...

DENNIS. Thought I was being, you know, careful.

LAUREN *shakes her head.*

LAUREN. Fuck's sake, Dad.

DENNIS. Stayed right by the, by the edge. And I hardly, I mean, I was very sort of quiet.

LAUREN. Sick of this.

DENNIS. Sick of what?

LAUREN. Tiptoeing around you all the time. Cos you're all sad and, and struggling. Which is...

I know you've lost your wife, Dad. And that is shit. That is so hard.

But the thing is: I've lost someone too. I've lost my mum. That is also shit. That is also hard.

Quite a lot to manage, if I'm honest, without having to worry about you and all.

DENNIS. I've not done it on purpose, love.

LAUREN. You have done it though.

DENNIS. Just thought –

LAUREN. Not a lot of evidence of thinking, Dad. If I'm honest. Now Ed's probably losing his job. At quite a crucial time for

us two, actually. When we could really do with him having a
job. But it's not your fault – never is – you just didn't think.

DENNIS. Why's it crucial? A crucial time?

LAUREN. Doesn't matter.

DENNIS. If you need some money, I've got, you know. Got a
bit put away. Rainy day.

LAUREN. That's not true.

DENNIS. Well I'd find some.

LAUREN. We're not stuck for money, Dad. I'm just. Well. I'm
pregnant, so...

We had the scan on Thursday. Everything's fine. Six months
you'll be a grandad.

DENNIS. Pregnant?

LAUREN. Yes, Dad. And obviously this isn't how I imagined
telling you, thought Ed would make us a nice vegan stew
which we'd tell you was a shepherd's pie cos we've got to be
careful, haven't we? Don't want to blow your mind with
lentils. Thought we could like focus on the positives,
celebrate the miracle of life, together, get excited, together.
But you've shat on that now, haven't you? Completely.

DENNIS *looks very wounded.*

A moment.

DENNIS (*defeated*). I'll head home, I think.

LAUREN *sighs.*

DENNIS *leaves.*

ANGIE *looks at* LAUREN. *She doesn't know what to say.*

LAUREN *makes an exasperated noise.*

LAUREN. That went well.

A moment.

Might just need a minute to...

ANGIE. Alright, love.

ANGIE *watches her. Checks she's alright.*

LAUREN *stands a second. She breathes in. She breathes out.*

She picks up her guitar.

She plays 'Let Him Fly' by The Chicks.

ANGIE *listens.*

LAUREN *puts the guitar down again.*

Autumn

5.

The 'Recent Sightings' board is filled in:

'AVOCET
BRENT GEESE
REDSHANK'

ANGIE *wheels the sign in, closes the door.*

LAUREN *is sitting down. She's just had a contraction.*

ANGIE. How long?

    LAUREN *looks at the time on her phone.*

LAUREN. Seventeen minutes.

ANGIE. He'll be kicking himself he's not here yet.

LAUREN. Needs to check his phone then, doesn't he? Left him about six voicemails. Starting to wish the bloke from giffgaff was the dad.

ANGIE. He'll be on his way.

LAUREN. Lovely accent.

ANGIE. Just be down the point or something.

LAUREN. No signal. No sense of urgency. Thinking about lapwings, not a care in the world.

ANGIE. He'll be here, love.

LAUREN. Been working so much. Phone on silent, no distractions, long long hours, trying to prove he cares. And, thing is: he's not even technically late yet. Double-checked the website, you're not meant to go in till they're every five minutes.

ANGIE. The website doesn't realise you live thirty miles away.
  On quite a windy road. With Ed sticking to the speed limit.
  In a Fiat Panda.

LAUREN. I'll give him another ring.

  LAUREN *does*.

  She puts the phone down, shakes her head.

ANGIE. I'll text your dad as well.

LAUREN. My dad is the last thing we need – isn't he though?
  Crashing in, panicking, making stuff much, much worse.
  Like he does.

ANGIE. Lauren.

LAUREN. Barely spoken for months. But I'm actually fine with
  that. I actually… There's been a lot of times where we
  could've done and we haven't so…

ANGIE. Need someone to keep an eye on things while I find Ed.

  ANGIE *texts* DENNIS.

  Is it worth thinking some calm thoughts?

LAUREN. Calm. Thoughts?

ANGIE. What's the calmest you've been?

LAUREN. Not this.

ANGIE. Have you not got a sort of, calm place?

LAUREN. Have you?

ANGIE. Oh, yeah. Yep.

LAUREN. Tell me about it then.

ANGIE. Think it works better if it's your calm place. Not sure
  you can borrow mine.

LAUREN. Just till Ed gets here. Please.

ANGIE. Oh. Okay. Um.

  So… we're on the beach. Kilnsea beach.

LAUREN. I'm shutting my eyes but I'm listening.

ANGIE. This is, this is twenty years ago now and. I've not been sleeping well really. Just cos of, various things.

I can get off to sleep alright but I wake up early, before the sun's up, usually.

So, um, I've started going for a little walk, on the beach, while nobody's around. Just sort of gather my thoughts, while the light comes, the daylight comes.

Is this...?

LAUREN. Keep going.

ANGIE. And this morning, it's not sunny but it's the first time, first time I've noticed anyway, stuff's a bit less gloomy. Like something's lifted a bit, weather-wise. There's usually a day, isn't there, where you notice it's spring? And it's today. So I'm feeling a bit less... I don't know, anyway. And then, up the beach, I see this... Don't know what it is to begin with. I mean I know it's a bird but just, don't know what kind of... Just notice it's. Well.

Big.

Sort of: properly big.

To be honest I couldn't believe it was staying in the air, but it was, just gliding. Slow, quiet, not in a hurry at all.

And, yeah. Beautiful.

Felt like it changed the world a bit, just by sort of passing through it. Like the air around it slowed its pace, deep breaths, found a new rhythm. Peaceful.

Just stood over there, watched.

Watched it fly the length of Kilnsea beach – glide, really – then away, down Spurn or out to sea, I don't know.

No one else about. Just me.

And it's strange, meant to be bad luck, isn't it, an albatross? Like an omen or, dunno. But I think really it was just what I needed. Just right. Just the thing.

So that's.

Those are my calm thoughts.

If they help.

A moment.

DENNIS *enters.*

DENNIS. Everything alright?

ANGIE. Dennis, I need you to listen.

She looks at LAUREN.

LAUREN. I've started.

DENNIS. Fucking hell, love, are you – ?

LAUREN. I'm fine. I mean it's not the most comfortable I've ever been, but it's only early days. That said, I would feel better if we could get hold of Ed.

DENNIS. Tried ringing him?

LAUREN. We had thought of that, Dad, yes.

DENNIS. Course.

LAUREN. He's either ignoring me, focusing on the last good Saturday of birdwatching – and I can understand why, I'm fairly low-maintenance, not like anything big's happening that he is at least in some way responsible for –

ANGIE. Or…?

LAUREN. Or he's somewhere with no signal, worrying about migration.

ANGIE. Can you think where he might be?

DENNIS. Canal Scrape I reckon. Been a lot of people there today. Lot of excitement about a tundra bean goose.

ANGIE. I'll go look for him there.

ANGIE *sets off.*

A moment.

LAUREN *doesn't make it easy for* DENNIS.

DENNIS. Well.

LAUREN. Well what?

DENNIS *isn't sure.*

DENNIS. Dunno.

LAUREN *looks at him.*

I don't.

LAUREN. Maybe be quiet then.

DENNIS. Lauren.

LAUREN. Is that being quiet?

DENNIS. No. Sorry.

A moment.

LAUREN. I'm absolutely livid with Ed.

Like of all the times to be not answering your phone.

A moment.

DENNIS *doesn't know what to say.*

He looks at LAUREN. *Pulls a 'what-is-he-like?' face.*

A moment.

(*Quite a long one.*)

Her guard comes down a bit.

Don't know if I can do this, Dad.

DENNIS. Oh, love.

He pats her a bit.

You definitely can.

A moment.

Also, you've started now, best to just keep going.

LAUREN. Cheers.

DENNIS. That's what being a mum is, I think. You start and then you just keep going.

And being a dad.

LAUREN. Not even started pushing.

DENNIS. I wouldn't yet.

LAUREN. This is so like Ed.

DENNIS. Be worth it. Promise.

LAUREN. Don't.

DENNIS. Got such a lovely life, all together, ahead of you.

I can see it.

So don't be worried. Be excited, if you can.

I'm excited.

LAUREN. You don't have to squeeze it out of your –

DENNIS. No, I don't, I know.

LAUREN. To be honest: I am absolutely shitting myself.

DENNIS. What would your mum say?

LAUREN *shrugs*.

He hugs her.

You're doing really, really well, and I love you.

A moment.

LAUREN. Yeah she would've said that actually.

DENNIS. Trained me well. Sometimes.

A moment.

Look I know I've been shit and this maybe isn't the best time to talk about it –

LAUREN. You think?

DENNIS. But I just need to say: I'll do better.

LAUREN. Dad.

DENNIS. We can talk about stuff. About your mum really.

Don't need to hide stuff. Her guitar. How sad you are. From me.

Cos, I'd hate you to be hiding stuff. I'd hate you to be sad, not tell me.

But I know you've had to. You have.

LAUREN *doesn't know what to say. She shrugs.*

LAUREN. Bit.

DENNIS. I'm sorry. I am.

LAUREN. Dad.

DENNIS. Maybe you can sing to it? Once it's out.

Maybe that's a plan?

Your mum always used to do that to you. Rubbed off a bit.

LAUREN. Maybe.

LAUREN *smiles at* DENNIS.

ED *arrives, out of breath.*

ED. Oh em gee I am so so sorry, Lauren. Are you okay?

LAUREN. Yeah no biggie, Ed, don't worry, I'm just literally going into labour but you carry on looking at your birds.

ED. I am honestly, mortified.

LAUREN. Good. Let's go.

ED. Car's outside, and I've got the bag and that.

LAUREN *gets up,* ED *helps.*

LAUREN. Thanks, Dad.

ED. Dennis, thanks so much. We'll keep you posted, obvs.

DENNIS *nods.*

DENNIS. Best get going.

They leave.

We hear ED *drive off.*

DENNIS *is left by himself.*

He looks around at the empty café.

Takes it all in.

A moment.

ANGIE *arrives.*

DENNIS. Found him then.

ANGIE. He was on his way back anyway actually. Bit of a hurry. I didn't try keeping up.

She smiles at DENNIS.

Strange to think, really.

DENNIS. Them being on their way?

ANGIE *nods.*

ANGIE. Very slowly, I should imagine, paying quite careful attention to the speed limits.

DENNIS *laughs.*

DENNIS. No hurry, I suppose.

ANGIE. Until Ed suddenly experiences Lauren having a contraction for the first time, maybe just the other side of Easington, inches up the speedometer a bit.

DENNIS. Maybe thirty-five?

ANGIE. Right. Pasty.

DENNIS. I'm not hungry, to be honest, Angie. Nothing against your pasties, obviously just... you know.

ANGIE. Lot to think about. Lot going on.

DENNIS. Maybe I can help with...?

DENNIS *gestures to the café, which has lots of trays of dirty pots.*

ANGIE. Don't worry about this, love.

DENNIS. I'm a good washer-upper. I mean I'm alright. Well. Not great but I've not got anything else to do.

ANGIE. Oh. Well. Alright. Cheers.

DENNIS *carries a tray of pots into the kitchen.*

DENNIS (*off*). Fill in for Lauren tomorrow as well, if it's…

A moment.

DENNIS *reappears.*

Can't leave you on your own on your last day.

ANGIE *smiles.*

And anyway: keep me out of trouble.

ANGIE. What trouble are you planning tomorrow?

DENNIS. They've opened up the photography competition again. Neil's lent me his camera. Which is very decent of him, actually, I know.

He's not entering this year. Reigning champion.

Given me a bit of advice though.

But I know it's, it's a bad idea. After last year. With the trampling and that. Ed getting into trouble. Me having to tell them it was me. Which was, you know. Not my finest hour if I'm honest.

ANGIE. Not your finest.

DENNIS. Better off in here. Also, keep my mind off what's happening with Lauren, won't it? There's nothing I can do, I know, I just…

ANGIE *picks up a tray and carries on.*

ANGIE. Well, I can always use an extra pair of hands.

6.

The 'Recent Sightings' board is the same as yesterday.

ANGIE *fetches the sign in, leans it against the wall, closes the door.*

She sighs.

DENNIS *appears from the kitchen, in quite a colourful apron.*

DENNIS. I'd've done that.

    ANGIE *shakes her head.*

ANGIE. Last time and everything.

DENNIS. You sad?

    ANGIE *thinks.*

ANGIE. The chiller cabinet's on its last legs. It's been touch-and-go every time I've switched it on for about three years. Not sure it'd've kept going much longer.

DENNIS. I've quite enjoyed it.

ANGIE. Well I'm sure whoever's running the Discovery Centre next year will be very happy to give you a job.

DENNIS. Maybe.

ANGIE. Write you a reference.

DENNIS. Oh.

ANGIE. Worked for me for one day, burnt every single teacake, broke two mugs –

DENNIS. Three now.

    He shows ANGIE *a broken mug.*

ANGIE. You'll want to be at home, in case you hear anything?

DENNIS. Rather be here.

    ANGIE *looks at* DENNIS.

ANGIE. It's ever so normal, isn't it, to have a little bit of time in the incubator?

DENNIS. Just means they're keeping an eye on things. And if they find anything, she's in the right place. It will be alright.

DENNIS *has reassured* ANGIE *a bit, and himself a bit.*

Ed'll be home for the night soon.

ANGIE. Must be a good sign they've sent him home.

DENNIS. Probably sick of him.

ANGIE *smiles.*

ANGIE. Wonder how Lauren's doing?

DENNIS *looks a bit lost.*

Well, this'll take a bit to get cleared up, sorted. I've got a couple of old crates, found them on the beach but they've cleaned up alright, thought I'd put some of the pots I'm keeping in those. And it'd be nice to give everywhere a good, a proper mop before I go home so you're welcome to stick around here, I'll be a couple of hours.

DENNIS *nods.*

DENNIS. Bit more washing up.

He goes back into the kitchen.

ANGIE *gets the crates to pack, with things she's keeping.*

She sees ED *approaching.*

ANGIE. Ed's here, Dennis.

ED *arrives.*

Hiya, love. Come here.

ANGIE *gives him a massive hug.* DENNIS *appears.*

DENNIS. Any news?

ED. They're both alright, doing a bit better actually, I think. Things are, well, settling, a bit.

DENNIS. Is the little one – ?

ED. Still keeping an eye on her, for tonight anyway, just cos, breathing-wise she was a bit sort of wobbly to begin with. But like, we all take a little while to get the hang of stuff, don't we? I do, anyway. For example: quinoa.

ANGIE. And how's Lauren?

ED. She's a flipping legend. Isn't she though? Bit knackered, obvs, and a bit… But alright. And I'm just completely so proud of her. Both of them.

I've got a photo.

ED *shows* ANGIE *and* DENNIS *his phone. They both melt.*

ANGIE. Oh, love.

DENNIS. Quite hairy, isn't she?

ANGIE. Dennis.

DENNIS. I just mean: she's got quite a lot of hair. For a newborn. Good hair.

ED *nods and smiles.*

ANGIE. Beans on toast?

ED. Oh, Angie, that'd be…

DENNIS. I can get it.

ANGIE. You absolutely can't.

ANGIE *goes into the kitchen for a bit.*

A moment.

DENNIS *doesn't really know what to say to* ED.

ED. Neil said he lent you his camera.

DENNIS. Just for a bit.

ED. Any good photos?

DENNIS. Not thought about it much today, if I'm honest.

ED *smiles. He looks worried though.*

A moment.

I think I should just say now: you'll be a really good dad.

ED. Um.

DENNIS. You will.

And this bit, the very first bit... Remember feeling, quite daunted.

By the task in hand.

Cos they're just... very little. And, er. Fragile. Aren't they?

But you don't need to be. Daunted.

You'll be very good at it.

ED. Do my best.

DENNIS. You will.

And that is coming from...

I've been quite average at it.

If I think about it, I've got some things wrong and got some things right. So yeah. Somewhere in the middle.

And Lauren's turned out, you know. Pretty, pretty good, hasn't she?

ED. I think so.

DENNIS. And mostly that was... She had a really good mum, but. I am a bit... I do think, partly, I like to think a bit of that was me.

ED *nods.*

And if I can do it. Me. Then I really think...

A moment.

ED *is on the edge of tears.*

ED. Just wanted to help, a bit. And I couldn't. While it was all happening, while Lauren was... And then they, quite quickly they had to put her, put the little one in a, thingy, incubator thingy, it all felt a bit...

It is just so… I dunno. Hard. Isn't it? Grown up and proper and just, really, really…

ED *is upset.*

DENNIS *gives* ED *a hug.*

A moment.

DENNIS. You'll be right. Alright? Good at looking after stuff. As long as there's no idiots.

ED *is calmer.*

He gets a text message.

ED. Sorry, I'll just, in case it's…

He looks at his phone.

Dennis: you absolutely have to go to the beach. Now.

DENNIS. Still drying up.

ED. I promise it's worth it, I promise. Grab the camera. Go.

ED *picks up* DENNIS*'s camera, puts it round* DENNIS*'s neck.*

Go.

He bundles DENNIS *out of the door.*

ANGIE *appears with some beans on toast.*

ANGIE. What's…?

ED *shows* ANGIE *the text on his phone.*

ANGIE. Crikey.

ED. He better get a photograph.

ANGIE. Go too.

ED. Think this one's just Dennis's.

ANGIE *nods.*

Also, I'm knackered. Like I know Lauren has done so much more but… And then, bit of a, a worrying day as well. Knocked us for six a bit.

ANGIE. Here.

ANGIE *gives* ED *his beans on toast.*

ED. Thank you.

ANGIE *smiles.*

She is magic though. You can see her getting the hang of things already. Like sort of: stretching out and stuff. Opening her eyes. And she's just like: 'Wow, I love it.'

ED *smiles. Then looks a bit worried. He says this to his beans:*

Angie, I've got something to ask you. But before I ask you, I have to say it is absolutely fine to say no, if it doesn't feel right or...

ANGIE *isn't sure what to make of this.*

ANGIE. Right.

ED. It's a bit...

ANGIE. Okay.

ED. So we're thinking about names, me and Lauren. And for her middle name we're going to call her Victoria, after Lauren's mum, cos, dunno, just want to. Lauren said her mum would've made out we were being daft or something, soppy, but then secretly been chuffed.

ANGIE. She definitely would.

ED. So that's her middle name. But then for her first name we wondered – and if it doesn't feel right, you just have to say, please – but we were thinking maybe of calling her, um, Jenny? She just, she looks like a Jenny, don't know what it is, we both saw her and like had the same thought. And maybe it'd be nice to... But maybe it wouldn't and, I dunno. We don't want to do it if it makes you sad.

ANGIE*'s a bit tearful.*

Which, um, it is doing, so. Don't give it another thought, we'll just... Glad we checked.

ANGIE. No, love, not sad just. Took me by surprise a bit.

ED. Oh.

ANGIE. In a, a lovely way.

ED. Oh.

> ANGIE *gathers herself a bit.*
>
> *Shrugs. Smiles.*

ANGIE. If she's a Jenny, she's a Jenny.

> ED *smiles.*

ED. Think maybe she is a Jenny.

> *A moment.*

ANGIE. Can't wait to meet her.

ED. You're our number-one babysitter, Angie. Be sick of the sight of her.

ANGIE. Take a while, I think.

ED. Right. Jenny. Jenny Victoria.

> ED *looks at his beans.*
>
> I don't know if I can finish this, Angie, sorry.

ANGIE. Maybe time for a nap, is it?

> ED *smiles.*

ED. Maybe.

ANGIE. Let me know how they're doing, won't you?

ED. Course.

> ANGIE *gives* ED *a big hug.*

ANGIE. Sleep tight.

> ED *leaves.*
>
> ANGIE *clears his plate, bins what's left of his beans on toast. He hasn't eaten much.*
>
> *She takes a moment, just to think about there being another Jenny in the world.*

And then she goes back to packing things up.

DENNIS *enters.*

He is smiling, shaking his head.

DENNIS. Angie.

ANGIE. Saw it then?

DENNIS. Just soaring past. Slow. Graceful. Exactly like you said.

ANGIE *smiles.*

ANGIE. Please tell me you got a photo.

DENNIS *shakes his head, still smiling.*

What?

DENNIS. Just thought: can't keep it in a photograph. Wouldn't want to anyway. Keep it in here instead.

He points at his head.

Keep it in here.

His heart.

And I will.

DENNIS *looks at* ANGIE. *They smile.*

DENNIS *has given up on asking* ANGIE *out.*

(*Although now would be a very good moment.*)

ANGIE *sees this.*

She makes a decision.

ANGIE. Think I'll leave this for tomorrow actually.

DENNIS. Oh.

ANGIE. Shall we just nip to the pub?

DENNIS. We can sort it tonight.

ANGIE. Still be here in the morning. I fancy a drink. D'you fancy a drink?

DENNIS. Oh. Well. If you're... I do, really.

ANGIE. I fancy a...

Deep breath.

Like a this-could-be-the-start-of-something drink? If that makes sense.

DENNIS *smiles, nods.*

DENNIS. Think so.

ANGIE. Lovely. Let's do that then.

7.

The bow.

LAUREN *comes on first, playing the intro to 'Some Days You Gotta Dance' by The Chicks on the guitar.*

ED *arrives, pushing a pram, with Jenny in.*

ANGIE *and* DENNIS *enter.*

LAUREN *sings, and the others line dance.*

The End.